CONTENTS

BE A BUSY BEE

Hi, honey child, I'm Benjamin Bee.
I've got loads of things for you to see,
Things to make and things to do,
Cakes to eat and prezzzents too.
Pumpkin surprises and cheeky chicks,
Things for Easter and Halloween tricks,
Flowers for Mom and spooky candy,
And a picnic cloth that will come in handy…

Most things are eazzzy, use paint and a brush,
Read the instructions and try not to rush.
But some things are harder, and then you'll be glad
To call on your mom, or even your dad.
I'll tell you when you need someone there,
So don't ever panic, never despair,
Remember the words of Benjamin Bee.

Follow my lead and stick with me,
I'll show you how, just wait and see.
I'm always bizzzy, I'm a bizzzy bee.
Do you think you can be as bizzzy as me?

EASTER CHICKY CHUMS

Use wild colors on these cheeky little chicks, and have fun with their floaty tissue tails.

You will need:

- 4 raw eggs
- Darning needle
- Bowl
- Wooden skewer
- Colored paints
- Paintbrush
- Colored tissue paper
- Tracing paper
- Pencil
- Thin yellow cardboard
- Scissors
- Glue

Shapes to trace

Template for small wing
Cut 8

Template for large wing
Cut 8

Template for beak
Cut 4

Template for feet
Cut 4

How to make the chicks

1 Ask your mom or dad to blow four eggs. To do this, make a hole in the top and bottom of each egg with a darning needle. Carefully holding the shell over a bowl, blow hard into one hole and the egg will come out of the other hole.

Benjamin Bee says...

"Grownups! When blowing eggs, the bigger the hole, the easier it will be. But be careful because if it is too big, the egg will break."

2 When the shells are dry, place them on wooden skewers and paint them. For the chicks' feathery heads, scrunch up small balls of red tissue paper. Glue four down the back of each egg. Now trace around the beak template and transfer it to the thin yellow cardboard. Cut out the shape, fold it in half, and then glue it to the egg, very gently…

3 Trace around the templates for the wings. For each egg, cut two large wings out of red tissue paper and two small wings out of blue. Glue the blue on top of the red and stick the wings to each side of the eggs. Now tear 12 leaf-shaped strips of colored tissue. Glue three strips to the bottom of each egg so that they point upwards.

4 Paint the eyes—a white circle first and then a dot of black. Next, trace around the feet template and transfer to yellow cardboard. Cut out four sets of feet. Carefully glue one to the base of each egg.

CELEBRATION TREE

Cute cone baskets filled with chocolate treats make pretty tree decorations for festivals and celebrations.

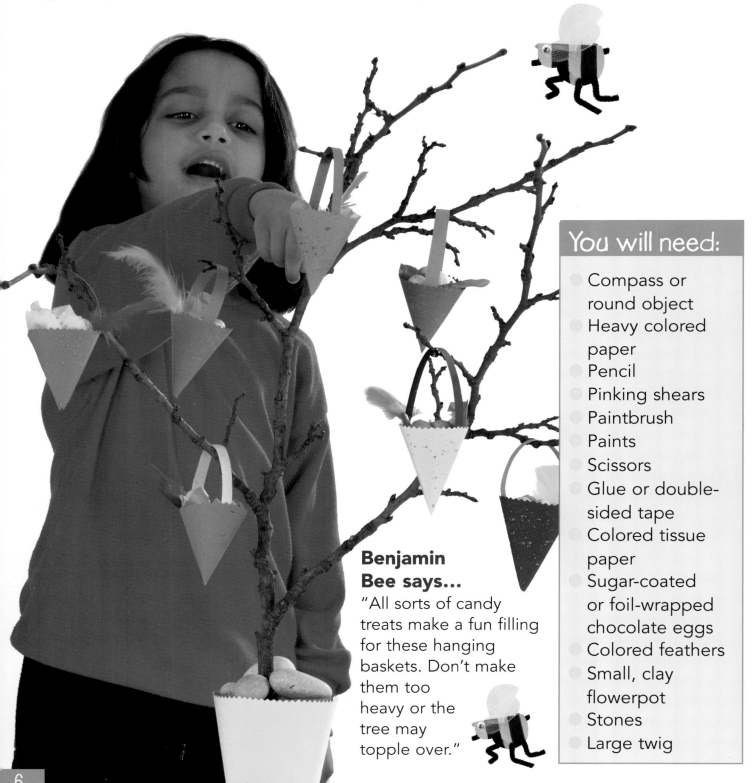

Benjamin Bee says...

"All sorts of candy treats make a fun filling for these hanging baskets. Don't make them too heavy or the tree may topple over."

You will need:

- Compass or round object
- Heavy colored paper
- Pencil
- Pinking shears
- Paintbrush
- Paints
- Scissors
- Glue or double-sided tape
- Colored tissue paper
- Sugar-coated or foil-wrapped chocolate eggs
- Colored feathers
- Small, clay flowerpot
- Stones
- Large twig

1 Use a compass or draw around a circular object on colored paper to make seven 6-in. circles. Cut them out using pinking shears to make a zigzag edge. Cut seven strips of colored paper, ½ in. x 7 in., for the handles.

2 Dip a stiff-bristled brush into paint and draw back the bristles with a fingernail to spatter the circles with different-colored paints.

3 Cut away just over a quarter of each circle. Roll the paper into a cone and stick the overlapping edges with glue or double-sided tape. Stick a handle to the inside edge of each side of the cones.

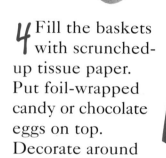

4 Fill the baskets with scrunched-up tissue paper. Put foil-wrapped candy or chocolate eggs on top. Decorate around the edges with brightly colored feathers.

5 Lay the flowerpot down on colored paper. Roll it along, marking next to the top and bottom of the pot with a pencil. Allow a 2-in. overlap. Cut out with pinking shears and wrap around the pot. Glue the edge. Weigh down the pot with a few stones. Wedge in a large twig and secure with more stones. Hang the baskets from the twig.

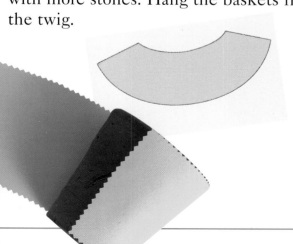

Benjamin Bee says...

"Why not make the baskets out of white paper and then paint them with different colors? Add some glitter, too!"

MOTHER'S DAY FLOWERS

Make these dazzling paper daffodils as a special gift for your mom or grandma. They look great, don't need water, and won't ever wilt!

You will need:

- Tracing paper
- Pencil
- Yellow and orange tissue paper
- Scissors
- Garden wire, 36 in. per stem
- Green crêpe paper
- Tape
- Thin yellow and green cardboard
- Double-sided tape or glue

Template for daffodil

4½ in.

1½ in.

1 To make one daffodil trace around the daffodil template. Sandwich three layers of yellow tissue together and transfer the outline to the top layer. Cut out the three layers together.

2 For the stem, bend a 36-in. length of wire into three. Twist these three strands together. Push the stem through the middle of all three tissue flowers and bend the wire slightly to secure.

3 Cut a ¾-in. wide strip from one edge of a roll of green crêpe paper. Tape one end of the crêpe strip to the stalk. Wrap it around the rest of the stalk a few times until it is thickly covered. Tape the end to the stalk.

4 To make the inside of the daffodil, cut a 4½-in. x 1½-in. rectangle of thin yellow cardboard. Roll it into a tube and secure it with double-sided tape or glue. Make ½-in. snips around one edge and fold them back.

5 Stick a piece of double-sided tape across the unfrayed end of the tube, sticking the ends to the inside of the tube. Stick the tube onto the middle of the paper petals. Stuff scrunched-up orange tissue paper inside the tube. Bend the stalk a little just below the flower.

6 To make two more daffodils, repeat steps one to five twice. Then cut long, thin leaf shapes out of thin green cardboard. Arrange the leaves and flowers in a vase.

CATERPILLAR CAKE

Have you seen any hairy, green caterpillars on the summer plants? Well here's one you can't miss—and it tastes good, too!

You will need:

- Bowls, wooden spoon, tablespoon, fork, spatula, muffin pan, plate
- ¾ cup butter or margarine
- ¾ cup fine ground sugar
- 3 medium eggs
- 1¾ cups self-rising flour
- Paper cupcake cases

Benjamin Bee says...

If you don't have self-rising flour, make your own by adding 1½ teaspoons baking powder and ½ teaspoon salt to a cup of all-purpose flour.

For the icing and decoration

- Raspberry jam
- 2¾ cups confectioners' sugar, sifted
- ¾ cup butter
- Green food coloring
- Green laces, strawberry sticks and assorted candy

1 Heat the oven to 170°C /325°F. Cream the butter and sugar together in a bowl with a wooden spoon. Lightly beat the eggs with a fork in another bowl, then mix these into the butter and sugar mixture. Fold in the flour.

2 Place at least 15 paper cases into a muffin pan (you may need two or three pans). Using a tablespoon, spoon a little mixture into each case. Ask an adult to put the pan in the oven. Bake for 20–25 minutes, or until lightly browned.

3 Leave the cakes to cool. Peel away the paper cases. Place six cakes upside down on a plate and spread the bases with raspberry jam. Top with another six cakes. Use three cakes to make the head and stack them one on top of the other. Trim them slightly to make an even shape.

4 Make the icing. Beat the butter and confectioners' sugar together. Mix in a few drops of food coloring. Spread over the cakes with a spatula.

5 Use the green laces to make the legs, and the strawberry sticks for the antennae. Add candy for the eyes and decoration.

COOL COOKIES

They're fun to make, crazy and colorful to look at and delicious to eat! Enjoy these beautiful iced bugs.

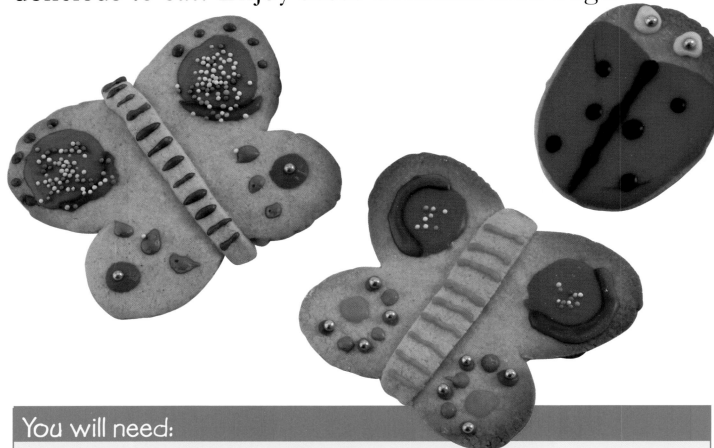

You will need:

Utensils
- Tracing paper
- Pencil

- Thin cardboard
- Scissors
- Bowls
- Wooden spoon
- Fork
- Rolling pin
- Knife
- Non-stick baking pan
- Piping bag

For the cookies
- ½ cup soft butter
- ½ cup fine ground sugar
- 1 medium egg
- 3½ cups sifted flour

For the icing
- ¾–1 cup confectioners' sugar
- Food coloring: red, green, orange, blue, white, black (or use colored icing in tubes)
- Sprinkles and edible silver balls

1 Heat the oven to 180°C/350°F. Trace around the butterfly and ladybug templates. Transfer the outlines to thin cardboard and cut out.

2 Mix the butter and sugar together with a wooden spoon. Crack the egg into a bowl and mix together the yolk and white. Add the egg, a little at a time, to the butter and sugar mixture. Add the flour and stir well to form a dough. Knead the dough into a ball with your hands.

Template for ladybug

4 Place the templates on the dough and cut around them with a knife. Put your shapes on a non-stick baking pan. Add dough strips for the butterfly bodies. Bake the cookies in the oven for about 10 minutes, or until browned. Remove and leave to cool.

Template for butterfly

5 Mix 1–2 tablespoons of water into the confectioners' sugar until it is thick enough to coat the back of a spoon. Divide the icing into batches and add a few drops of food coloring to each. Pipe icing designs onto the butterflies. Wash the bag each time you change colors (or use the icing tubes). Add some edible decoration.

3 Sprinkle some flour on the work surface. Roll out the dough with a rolling pin until it is ½ in. thick. Sprinkle a little flour over the surface of the dough as you work.

6 Spread red icing over the ladybugs. Pipe a few dots of black icing on the back and a long stripe down the body. Use white icing for the eyes and top them with silver balls.

TREASURE CHEST

Yo, ho, ho! Here's a pirate's treasure chest that's perfect for stashing all your candy treasures!

Benjamin Bee says...
"You can keep all sorts of goodies in your treasure chest, or put a present inside and give it to a very special friend!"

You will need:

- Cardboard box
- Scissors
- Ruler
- Glue
- Masking tape
- Tracing paper and pencil
- Thin cardboard
- Red and green paint
- Paintbrush
- Gold paint or marker
- Piece of felt
- Yellow paper

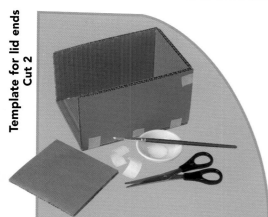

1 To make the chest, cut a 5-in. x 7-in. rectangle of cardboard for the base. Then cut two rectangles, 4 in. x 7 in., for the sides and two more, 4 in. x 4½ in., for the ends. Glue the four sides of the chest to the base, and use masking tape to secure until dry. Remove the tape.

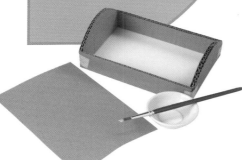

2 To make the lid, trace around the lid end template. Transfer to the cardboard and cut two. Now cut two long sides, 7 in. x 1 in. Glue them all together.

Tape together until dry. Cut a rectangle 7 in. x 6½ in. out of thin card to make the lid. Glue to the frame.

3 Remove the tape. Paint the outside of the chest and lid bright red. Paint the inside green. Leave to dry.

4 Trace around the template for the wavy edge. Transfer to yellow paper. Cut 12 strips to cover each edge of the treasure chest. Cut out, trim to fit and glue to all the edges.

5 Cut a strip of felt 6½ in. x 1 in. Glue one long edge of felt to the inside of one of the long edges of the chest. Glue the other long edge of felt to the inside long edge of the lid. Leave a small gap in the middle to allow the lid to open. Decorate the edging with gold dots and paint a gold keyhole on the front of the treasure chest.

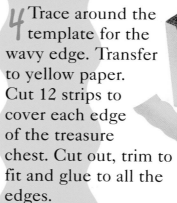

15

PICNIC PRINT CLOTH

Vegetable power! You can use peppers, mushrooms and okra to print this party-time picnic cloth.

Benjamin Bee says...
"To make different wacky prints, try a cauliflower cut in half, or a carrot, or an apple, or a pear..."

You will need:

- 2 peppers, okra and mushrooms
- Sharp knife
- Paintbrush
- 1 yd x 1¼ yd of plain cotton fabric
- Red, green, orange and blue fabric paint
- Flat plate
- Iron
- Pins and needle
- Red embroidery thread

1. **1** Ask your mom or dad to help you cut the vegetables in half. This must be done very neatly to make a flat surface to print with. Then ask them to iron the fabric and lay it flat on a hard surface.

2. **2** Put the different-colored paints on a flat plate. Add a little water if they are very thick. Use the paintbrush to coat the cut edge of the pepper with green paint. Starting in one corner, press the pepper firmly onto the cloth.

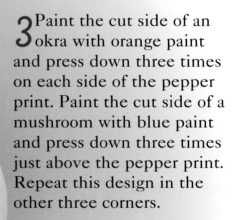

3 Paint the cut side of an okra with orange paint and press down three times on each side of the pepper print. Paint the cut side of a mushroom with blue paint and press down three times just above the pepper print. Repeat this design in the other three corners.

4 Create a design in the center of the cloth. Use the same vegetables but different colors. For the outer edge, make a pattern using the mushroom and the okra. Leave the cloth to dry.

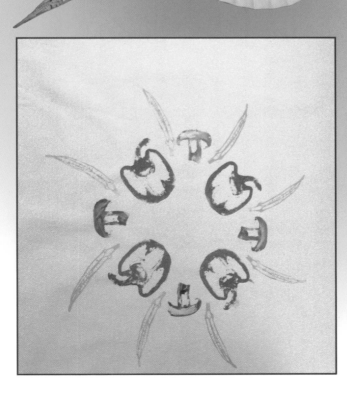

5 Fold under ½ in. of fabric all around the edge of the cloth. Ask an adult to iron the fold in place. Fold under another ½ in., then iron and pin in place. Thread the needle with red thread. Sew along the edge with running stitch. Now it's picnic time!

SMOOTHIE STRAWS

Make these fluttery straws from bits and pieces you have at home. Then enjoy a cooling summer smoothie.

Benjamin Bee says...
"You can use all sorts of fruit to make this drink. Banana or peach would taste good! Use the same quantities as shown for this one."

You will need:

For the straws:
- Pencil
- Tracing paper
- Thin cardboard or thick paper in green, yellow, blue and red
- Scissors
- Glue
- Colored pencils: red, blue, green
- 2 flexible straws
- Ruler

For two fruit smoothies:
- 1 cup mixed raspberries and strawberries
- Large glass bowl
- 1½ tablespoons sugar
- Food processor or blender
- Strainer
- Wooden spoon
- 1¼ cups milk
- 1 cup plain yogurt
- 2 tall glasses

For the straws

1 Trace around the templates for the butterfly and dragonfly. Transfer each onto a piece of folded colored paper. Place on the fold as indicated, and cut out. Unfold the shapes.

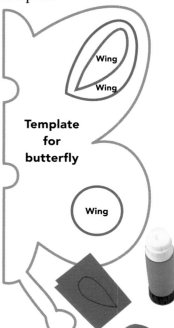

Template for butterfly

Wing
Wing
Wing

2 Trace around the wing decorations. Transfer these to folded paper and cut out, so you have identical pairs. Glue them to the wings of the butterfly and dragonfly as shown.

3 Using colored pencils, draw a striped pattern on the insect bodies and color in the eyes and feelers. Thread the insects onto two flexible straws. To make a lily pad mat for your glass, draw a circle about 3½ in. across onto green cardboard. Cut out. Cut a triangular wedge out of the circle and draw some lines from the center to the outside.

For the smoothies

1 To make the smoothie drink, put the fruit into the bowl and sprinkle on the sugar. Leave for 20 minutes, then puree the fruit in a food processor or blender.

2 Pour the mixture through a strainer into a clean bowl. Use a wooden spoon to press all of the juice out of the fruit. Stir in the milk and yogurt and mix again in the food processor or blender.

3 Pour the drink into two tall glasses. Place each glass on a lily pad and slurp it up with your super straws.

Template for dragonfly

Wing
Wing

WOBBLY POND SLIME

Ask your mom or dad to help you make this swampy jello for a party. Dig in—you never know what you'll find!

You will need:

- 1 can apricot halves
- 1 can pear halves
- 1 can peach halves
- Large glass bowl
- Heatproof jug
- 3 packs of green jello
- Boiling water
- Gummy candy
- Green licorice strings
- Marzipan
- Green food coloring
- Rolling pin
- Can opener
- Table knife

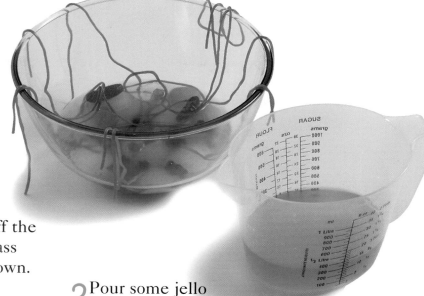

1 Open the cans of fruit and drain off the syrup. Cover the base of a large glass bowl with the fruit halves, cut side down. Ask an adult to make the green jello, according to the instructions on the box. Leave the jello to one side to cool a little.

3 Pour some jello over the fruit and candy to cover them. Leave to set slightly, then add more candy. Slowly pour more jello into the bowl until it is nearly full. Lower the ends of the licorice strings into the jello.

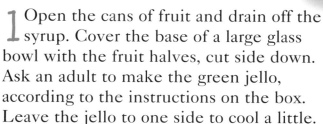

2 Meanwhile, scatter candy over the fruit and drape the licorice strings over the sides of the bowl.

Benjamin Bee says...
"This pond slime is great fun to eat! Choose sugar candy in lots of different shapes. You can buy fish, frogs and snakes to float in your pond."

4 Knead a drop of green food coloring into the marzipan until it is evenly colored. Roll out the marzipan to ½ in. thick. Use a knife to cut out three small circles. Cut a "V" shape out of each circle and use the knife to mark leaf veins. Place these on the jello. Scatter on more candy. Put in the fridge to set.

PUMPKIN SURPRISE

This papier mâché pumpkin, filled with candy, makes a great Halloween game to play with your friends!

You will need:

To make the paste:
- 2¼ cups all-purpose flour, sifted
- Bowl
- Water
- Fork

(or use wallpaper paste)

Plus:
- Large balloon, blown up
- Newspaper torn into strips
- Pin
- Poster paints: white, orange, black, brown
- Paintbrushes
- Pencil
- Craft knife
- Wrapped candy
- 1 yd nylon string
- 10-in. x 4-in. strip of thin green cardboard
- Glue
- Scissors
- Plastic stick

Making the paste

Put the flour into a bowl. Slowly add water, stirring with a fork, until the paste is as thick and smooth as mashed potatoes. Or just use wallpaper paste.

How to make the pumpkin

1 Tear the newspaper into strips. Dip a strip into the glue or wallpaper paste, then stick it onto the balloon. Keep pasting the strips until the balloon is covered with three layers of newspaper.

2 Leave the pumpkin to dry overnight. Use a pin to burst the balloon. Then paint the pumpkin with orange paint. Allow the paint to dry. You may need a second coat.

3 With a pencil, draw the outlines of the eyes, nose and mouth. Fill them in with black paint. When these have dried, paint thin brown lines from the top to the bottom, like the sections of a pumpkin.

4 Draw a circle (3 in. wide), at the top of your pumpkin. Ask your mom or dad to cut it out with a craft knife. Now get lots of your favorite candy and put it inside!

5 With a sharp pencil make a small hole 2 in. either side of the opening. Feed the ends of the nylon string through these holes and then pull the ends up through the center. Knot these ends together.

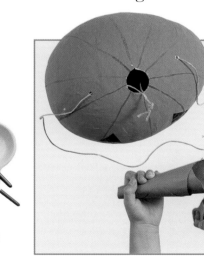

6 To make a stalk, roll the green cardboard into a cone, trim the top, and glue it. When this is dry, glue the stalk into the opening. Now hang the pumpkin up and you're ready to play. With a friend, take turns wearing a blindfold and bashing the pumpkin with a stick. Keep going. When the pumpkin breaks, the candy will fall out!

SPOOKY CANDIES

Scare your friends with these creepy-crawly candies. Make them any shade you like—just change the food coloring!

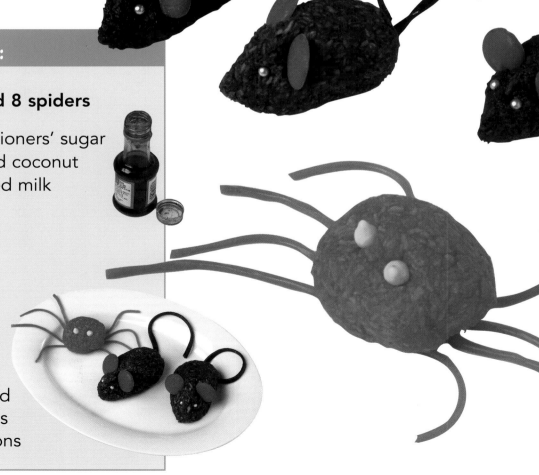

You will need:

Makes 8 mice and 8 spiders

- 1¾ cups confectioners' sugar
- 2 cups shredded coconut
- ⅔ cup condensed milk
- Mixing bowls
- Wooden spoon
- Black and red food coloring
- Toothpick
- Black and red licorice strings
- Edible silver balls and colored cake decorations
- Chocolate buttons

1 Put the confectioners' sugar, shredded coconut and condensed milk into a bowl. Mix together well using a wooden spoon.

2 Divide the mixture in half and put into two separate bowls. Add 2–3 drops of black food coloring to one bowl and 2–3 drops of red to the other. Knead the mixture with your hands to blend in the food coloring.

3 Mold small handfuls of black mixture into mouse shapes, and small handfuls of red mixture into round spider bodies. Use a toothpick to make a hole in the end of each mouse and insert a black licorice tail. For the spiders, make four holes along each side of their bodies. Cut two red licorice strings into four pieces each for the legs and insert.

4 Finally, push two silver balls into each mouse's face for eyes and add chocolate drops for ears. Use different-colored cake decorations for the spiders' spooky eyes.

POTATO WITCHES

Hubble, bubble…these witches are boiling up some trouble for Halloween. Are there any in your house!

Benjamin Bee says…
"You can also make long, thin carrot witches or short, fat turnip witches! Remember to change their clothes to fit!"

You will need:

- Knife
- 2 large, longish potatoes
- Green food coloring
- Paintbrush and dish
- Scissors
- Black felt
- Thumb tacks
- Black and green paper
- Black felt-tip pens
- Ruler and pencil
- Glue
- Twigs
- Pipe cleaners
- Green paint

1 Ask your mom or dad to cut off one end of each potato so it has a flat base. Use a paintbrush to cover the potatoes with green food coloring. Leave to dry.

2 For the witch's dress, cut a rectangle of black felt that wraps around the potato and overlaps slightly. Leave an overhang at the bottom and cut a zigzag pattern along the edge. Wrap around. Push thumb tacks through the fabric into the potato.

3 Cut a 2-in. x 4-in. rectangle of black paper to make the hair. Cut slits along one long edge, stopping ½ in. from the other long edge. Glue the uncut edge to the potato head. Draw a face on the potato using black felt-tip pen.

Template for witch's hat brim

Template for witch's cauldron

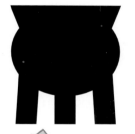

4 Trace the witch's hat cone and brim templates. Transfer to black paper and cut out. Roll the hats into cones and glue the straight edge down. Glue the cone to the potato. Mark the center of the brim piece. Cut slits, 1-in. long, from the center out. Trim the slit paper off to make a hole in the center of the brim. Push brims over the cones.

5 For the broom, push a 4-in. long twig into a bundle of thinner, 2-in. long twigs. Wrap a pipe cleaner around to secure. Glue to the witch's body. Make the other witch using green paper for the hair. Trace around the cauldron template, transfer to black paper and cut out. Add bubbling brew with green paint. Crease down the middle to make it stand.

Template for witch's hat cone

SNOW DOME

Even if it doesn't snow, you can make a glittering snow scene of your own and really shake up a storm!

1 Fill the jar two-thirds full with glycerine, then fill to the top with water. Add the glitter. Use a spoon to stir, and leave to settle.

2 Shape the clay into a lump that fits easily inside the jar lid, making sure it is flat on the top and the bottom. Ask Mom to help you bake the clay in the oven, following the instructions on the pack. Glue the ornament onto the clay, then glue the clay to the inside of the lid.

3 Hold the jar over a sink. Turn the lid and ornament upside down. Push the ornament into the liquid and screw the lid tightly onto the jar. Some of the liquid will overflow.

You will need:

- Small glass jar with a tight-fitting lid
- Glycerine
- Water
- Glitter
- Small spoon
- Oven-bake modeling clay
- Paintbrush for gluing
- Waterproof glue
- Small ornament, plastic or china
- Soft cloth

4 Use a soft cloth to wipe the outside of the jar clean. Shake the jar and see what a sparkling snowstorm you can make!

CHRISTMAS DECORATIONS

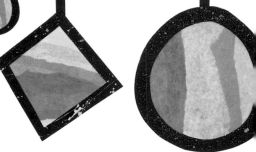

Design glowing jewels to hang at the window and colorful trees for your table.

For the tree chain you will need:

- Long strip of green paper
- Pencil
- Scissors

For the jewels you will need:

- Thin black cardboard
- White pencil
- Scissors
- Scrap paper or newspaper
- Stiff paintbrush
- Paints
- Colored tissue paper
- Glue

Benjamin Bee says...

To make a Xmas tree, fold a piece of thin cardboard in half and draw a tree with its pot. Cut out to make two trees. On one tree make a ½-in. cut from the base to the middle. On the other, cut from the top to the middle. Slot the two halves together so your Xmas tree stands up.

1 For the chain of trees, carefully fold your paper into a fan shape.

2 Draw a tree on the top fold. Cut out, leaving the branch tips uncut. Unfold, and presto—a chain of Xmas trees!

For the jewels

1 For the glowing jewels, use a white crayon to copy the tree shape onto black cardboard. Draw another tree, ¾ in. inside the first one. Use scissors to cut around the outside of the tree shape. Now cut out the center to leave a tree-shaped frame. Make a few more.

2 Lay the tree frames on some scrap paper or newspaper. Use a stiff paintbrush to splash paint onto the trees. To do this, pull the bristles back with your finger, and let go. Leave the trees to dry.

3 Tear up pieces of colored tissue paper. Stick the bits of tissue paper onto the back of the frames with watered-down glue. Make sure the pieces overlap, so that there are no gaps.

4 Cut a strip of black cardboard, ½ in. x 2½ in. Fold it in half to make a loop. Glue the loop to the tip of the tree, so that the folded end points upward. Trim away any extra tissue paper. Repeat with the other trees.

5 Use the loops to hang up your decorations. Put them against a window or on your Christmas tree, so that the light can shine through them. Now try making some other shapes.

GIFT TAGS

For really special Christmas presents,
add your own hand-made gift tags. Just trace these
templates, transfer to stiff white paper, cut out and color!

You will need:
- Templates
- Tracing paper
- Pencil
- Stiff white paper
- Scissors
- Felt-tip pens or paints
- Ribbon or string